Mind Maps®

for kids

tony buzan

THE INTERNATIONAL BESTSELLING AUTHOR

Mind Maps®
for kids

MAX your MEMORY and CONCENTRATION

with Susanna Abbott

 thorsons

Mind Map® is a registered trademark of The Buzan Organisation.

This edition produced for The Book People Ltd, Hall Wood Avenue, Haydock, St Helens WA11 9UL

Thorsons
An Imprint of HarperCollinsPublishers
77–85 Fulham Palace Road
Hammersmith, London W6 8JB

The website address is:
www.thorsonselement.com

and Thorsons are trademarks of
HarperCollinsPublishers Limited

First published by Thorsons 2005

10 9 8 7 6 5 4 3

© Tony Buzan, 2005

Tony Buzan asserts the moral right to
be identified as the author of this work

A catalogue record of this book
is available from the British Library

ISBN 9780007743858

Cartoons and Mind Map® illustrations by Stephanie Strickland

Printed and bound in Dubai by
Oriental Press.

Dedication

This book is dedicated to all the kids out there who dream of being able to remember everything they want, but haven't got the right formula to unlock their amazing memories and limitless creativity. This book contains that formula and will help you make all those dreams come true.

Acknowledgements

Many thanks to all the 'Master Mind Mapper' kids who have helped me with this book: Edmund Trevelyan-Johnson and Alexander Keene who used Mind Maps to help them get into the schools of their dreams; the pupils of Beechwood School in Slough who proved through Mind Maps what geniuses they all are; the children of Berryhill School in Scotland for their outstanding Mind Maps; the children of Willow Run School in Detroit; the children in Singapore's Learning and Thinking Schools; the children of Humano School in Leon, Mexico; the children of Seabrook Primary School in Australia; and all the other 'Mind Map' kids all over the world who I've been fortunate enough to meet!

With special thanks to my wonderful *Mind Maps for Kids* Support Team at Thorsons: Carole Tonkinson, Publishing Director; Susanna Abbott, Senior Editor, who has also helped me write and plan this book; Natasha Tait, Book Designer; Sonia Dobie, Cover Art Design Manager; Nicole Linhardt, Senior Production Controller; Liz Dawson, Publicity Manager; Laura Scaramella, Foreign Rights Director; and Belinda Budge, Managing Director.

A big thank you also to: Stephanie Strickland, Illustrator, who has helped bring this book alive with her outstanding illustrations; to Jo Godfrey Wood, Writer, for her help writing and planning this book; to Jenny Aviss, Principal of Wetherby Schools, for encouraging everybody to Mind Map; to Philip Nicholson of The King's School, Tynemouth, for his editorial advice; and to Caroline Shott, my incredible Literary Manager, whose energy, support and dedication constantly amaze me.

Finally, a special thank you to my *Mind Maps for Kids* Home Team: Lesley Bias for her 'flying fingers'; Vanda North for introducing kids around the world to the magic of Mind Maps; my brother, Professor Barry Buzan, for his decades-long support of me and the Mind Mapping concept; and to my mum, Jean Buzan, who has always encouraged this 'grown-up' Mind Map Kid!

Contents

Letter from Tony

What would you do if you could remember **anything** you wanted when **you** wanted? Would you:

- ★ *Become the world's expert on your favourite pop idol?*
- ★ **Impress** *your mates by knowing all the football scores this season?*
- ★ *Remember all the best jokes and become a* **celebrity** *comedian?*
- ★ *Learn everything about the stars and planets and become an* awesome *astronomer?*
- ★ *Become a* **famous** *actor and learn all your lines with ease?*
- ★ *Remember amazing events in history and become a* **brilliant** *explorer?*

When you can remember things well, you can achieve **anything** you want.

This book is all about helping you do just that. I'm going to teach you to use your memory to the **max** with my magic memory tools. Very soon you will find that you spend less time learning and more time **chilling**. You'll be strolling through your exams and will 'A'ce them all. You'll be the one who knows **everything** about your favourite interests and people will ask **YOU** to help them to remember things.

And the best thing of all? Using your memory is **fun**. Like you, your memory wants to **enjoy** itself and be **entertained**. When you learn how to play with your memory, you will see that **everything** is interesting – even if you think it's not right now. There are no limits to what you can learn and achieve. Armed with your **fantastic** memory you can make **ALL** your dreams come true.

So, what are you waiting for? Turn over the page and get ready to **max** your **Memory** and **Concentration!**

Your Marvellous Memory

Did you know that you have an infinite ability to remember **everything** and **anything** you want? Yes, ANYTHING!

Think about how much **easier** and more fun this makes life: you can impress your mates by knowing who scored what goal in any match your team has played; you won't be left high and dry if you forget your mobile as you'll know all your phone numbers; you'll get your facts **right** in exams because you'll remember everything you've learnt – think how easy this makes it to get the grades you **know** you deserve.

Before we get going, have a think about what **you** make of your memory. Do you reckon you have a 'good' memory or a 'bad' memory? Does it sometimes work **perfectly** but sometimes let you down? For example, when your teacher asks you a question in front of the whole class does the answer sometimes fail to spring to mind the second you need it? You know you know the answer really, it's on the tip of your tongue, but you just can't spit it out. Even more annoyingly, do you often find that, later on, when your brain has switched off and is thinking about something else, you suddenly remember the answer?

Why is this? If your memory ever lets you down it is not because you are being 'stupid' or 'slow' or any other of the negative labels you can dream up for yourself. All it means is that you need to give your memory a bit of **help** to store information, so that when you need it you can recall it.

Think of your brain as a **super-sized library**.

AMAZING BRAIN FACT
AN ELEPHANT NEVER FORGETS
Is it true that elephants have excellent memories? Yes! Most elephants can recognize human and animal friends after **YEARS** of separation: a group of young Tuli elephants recently returned to the wild in South Africa recognized each other and were **IMMEDIATELY** accepted back into their herds.

The information will **always** be there, but if it's all piled up in a big messy heap your memory will find it hard to remember it for you. What you need to do is help your brain store away information so that it is easy to access. This is what I'm going to help you with. By the time you finish this book, you will be the **master** of your memory and will be able to remember anything you want for as long as you want.

Mistress Mnemosyne

The word 'memory' comes from the name of the Greek goddess of memory – Mnemosyne (pronounced 'Nem-o-seen'). With the god Zeus she had nine children – the nine Muses. They grew up to be the goddesses of poetry about love, heroes, song, dance, comedy, tragedy, music, history and astronomy.

For the Greeks, it was the joining together of energy (Zeus) and memory (Mnemosyne) which produced creativity and knowledge (in the form of their children). This is true for you, too. If you use memory techniques, your memory will improve **and** you will also become more **creative**. This means that you will learn new things more quickly

AMAZING BRAIN FACT
THE MORE YOU KNOW, THE MORE IT GROWS

Your memory is like a muscle. The more you use it the stronger it gets and the easier it becomes to remember things. In fact, it even gets **BIGGER** so you can remember **MORE!** For example, taxi drivers in big cities have a larger hippocampus than most people because they have to memorize the routes they take around the city. (Hippo what? The hippocampus is part of the brain that works hard when you visualize things. It's shaped like a sea horse, which is how it got its name, from the Greek 'hippos', meaning horse, and 'kampos', meaning a sea monster.)

AMAZING BRAIN FACT
RECORD-BREAKING MEMORIES
The largest amount of playing cards **EVER** remembered
in the order they were shuffled is 54 packs – that's a
staggering 2,808 cards! The **AMAZING** memory behind
this record belongs to Dominic O'Brien from Great Britain,
eight-times winner of the World Memory Championships.
He was allowed to see each card once only before
repeating what he'd seen to the amazed judges.

Olympic Minds

Since the time of the Ancient Greeks, some people have made a big
impression on their friends by demonstrating the most **amazing** feats of
memory. For example, they have been able to remember hundreds of items
backwards and forwards and in any order – dates and numbers; names and
faces – and have been able to remember things like the order of packs of
shuffled playing cards **perfectly**!

How on **Earth (or the universe?)** is this possible? It may surprise you to know
that in most cases these people were using special Magic Memory Tools to
help them remember things.

These Magic Memory Tools all work using the two star players of your
memory:

1. **Imagination**
2. **Association**

If you want to remember anything you only have to associate (link) it to
something that you already know, using your imagination. **Imagination**
and **Association** make sure you score **every** time! Let's look at some of the
ways the two star players **Imagination** and **Association** help you get it right
every time.

BRAIN FLEXOR
JUGGLE THEM TOGETHER
Can you juggle? Juggling is not only **FUN** but is also a brilliant way of getting **BOTH** sides of your brain working together. Juggling will improve your memory and especially your concentration (see also pp.38–9).

Use Both Sides and Your Memory Will Fly!

Did you know that your brain is actually divided into two halves? The two halves of your brain have different functions and different ways of working. When you are thinking about things like words, numbers and lists you are exercising the **left** side of your brain. You give the **right** side of your brain a good workout when you notice colours, pick up the rhythm in your favourite song or use your imagination to dream up a theme for your birthday party.

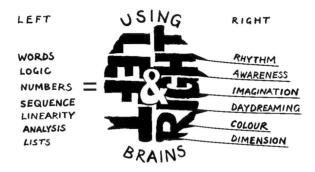

LEFT | USING | RIGHT

WORDS
LOGIC
NUMBERS = LEFT & RIGHT = RHYTHM
SEQUENCE AWARENESS
LINEARITY IMAGINATION
ANALYSIS DAYDREAMING
LISTS COLOUR
BRAINS DIMENSION

The reason why it's so important to use your imagination when you learn and remember things is because it gets the **right** side of your brain working hard, when normally you'd rely on the left. This can happen a lot at school because many of the things you need to learn – dates, facts and figures – are all favourites of the left brain. The thing is, using only one side of your brain is like trying to walk on one leg with your hand tied to your ankle: hard work! When you use both halves of your brain **together** as a team you won't just be able to walk more easily, you will be able to **sprint** to the finishing line – and beyond! It will be easier to remember **everything**.

1. Imagination

The thing about using your **imagination** to help you remember is that it makes everything **loads** more **interesting**. And the more interesting you find something, the easier it is to remember it. For example, here are two lists:

1. *Stone, blank, your, white, homework, with*
2. *Party, music, presents, holidays, presents, sunshine*

Which list is easier to remember? The one that **really** interests you or sounds more **fun**, of course. The things you don't like or which don't capture your **imagination** are so much easier to forget. The key is to use your **imagination** to make what you want to remember more interesting, even if you think it is boring. Let's look at the other players on the **Imagination** team:

★ **EXAGGERATION.** *OK, let's face it, the traditional method of crop rotation in the Middle Ages is not the most exciting thing to learn, but your* imagination *can make it much more interesting if you let it run* **wild.** *For example, imagine the crops at the end of each year jumping out of the soil and running* **madly** *across to the next field.*

★ **LAUGHTER.** *Laughter and jokes play on the same team as exaggeration. The more ridiculous and outrageous you make the image of what you are learning, the easier it will be to remember. So, as you imagine the crops sprinting into the next field, see the wheat puffing (ah! so that's where 'puffed wheat' came from!), sweating and out of breath.*

★ **SENSES.** *Use your five senses to help your* imagination *as much as possible. Imagine the fields as vividly as you possibly can.* **See the** *bright yellow ears of corn glowing in one field and feel how rough they are when you* **touch them;** **smell** *the damp earth;* **hear** *the scratch of the barley rubbing together in the third field;* **taste** *the sweet grains.*

★ **COLOURS.** *When you imagine the landscape, try to make the colours as* **vivid** *as possible. The gold of the wheat field is so* **bright** *that you turn to look at the dark soil in the empty field to rest your eyes; you then look across to the grassy-yellow barley moving in the breeze.*

WHAT'S CROP ROTATION ABOUT ANYWAY?

In the Middle Ages people changed the crops they planted in their fields each year so the soil wouldn't get worn out. One year they'd plant wheat, the next barley and for the third they'd plant nothing at all to let the soil rest, leaving it fallow.

★ **RHYTHM IS THE ANSWER.** *The more you get movement and rhythm involved with what you are learning, the more real the 'picture' will be in your mind. Imagine the crops running on their earthy roots as they* **zoom** *into the next field, the farmers sprinting up and down the strips of field to shepherd them across.*

★ POSITIVE THINKING. *In general, it is easier to remember things that you* **like** *and think of* **positively** *than things that you don't like or find negative. Instead of telling yourself that you mustn't forget something, tell yourself that you must* **remember** *it. If you start off worrying about forgetting, the chances are you will!*

AMAZING BRAIN FACT
A SHORT HISTORY OF THE BRAIN

Did you know:

★ The Earth is about ☞ **5,000,000,000** years old?

★ The first life on Earth began to appear about ☞ **4,000,000,000** years ago?

★ We developed our modern brain about ☞ **100,000** years ago?

★ We only figured out that our brains are in our heads not our hearts about ☞ **500** years ago?

And

★ We have discovered 95% of what we KNOW about what goes on in the brain in only the last ☞ **10** years?

What's more, scientists reckon that on average we use less than 1% of our brain's ability to remember things. Yes, less than 1%! Think of what that means for **you**! Think of how much **room** there is left over in the 99% of your brain you don't make use of – you really can memorize **anything** and **everything** you want!

Make sure you and your memory are always having FUN!

2. Association

What about the second star player for your memory? **Association** is all about the way you make **links** between what you know. For example, if you visit your old school, you might smell a certain smell, see something or hear something that immediately brings back a vivid memory from your time there. You can remember everything **perfectly**. The memory has been stored in your brain all the time and the smell or sound has acted as a **trigger** for your memory muscle to get working. Making **associations** like this is fun and easy as it gives you a chance to **flex** your **imagination**.

You can use this natural brain skill to your **advantage** to help you learn and remember things. **Association** is a bit like a massive wardrobe with hangers. If you want to learn something new, you need to find a connection between it and something already in your wardrobe and then put it on the same hanger.

Say you go to a party and meet somebody called Alex and want to remember his name. Your brother is also called Alex and he's an ace skateboarder. Imagine them both skating together on the **same** board. If you make a strong **association** between Alex at the party and your brother Alex you'll remember the new Alex, no sweat. What are the other players on the **Association** team?

★ **PATTERNS**. *Look for patterns in things you want to remember. Let's say you have to go to the shops for your parents and need to remember a shopping list. Try putting everything you need to buy in groups, e.g. fruit, vegetables, meat or household. This breaks down the information into smaller bite-sized pieces. Other patterns you can look for are: order of size (e.g. from big to small), order of things taking place (handy for remembering dates or events in order), colour groups, and so on.*

★ **NUMBERS**. *Numbering information in order can really help you remember lists of facts. There are special ways you can use numbers that we'll look at in Chapter 4.*

★ **SYMBOLS**. *Using symbols and pictures is another smart way of creating triggers for your memory. For example, every time you come up with a new idea you can draw a light bulb beside it, or if something has gone well, draw a smiley face alongside it. As you'll see in the next chapter, Mind Maps use lots of pictures and symbols.*

Now that you understand how to get the two star players of your memory, **Imagination** and **Association**, winning for you, it's time to take a look at some of the tools of the memory trade and get that **fantastic** memory of yours working to the **max**.

Memory
Mind
Maps

2

Mind Maps are the tool of choice to help you get your memory tuned. Mind Maps work so well because they work with the two star players of your memory: imagination and association.

The King of Memory Tools

Mind Maps are a special form of note-taking and planning that work **with** your brain to make it easier for you to remember things. They use **colour** and images to help get your **imagination** whirring and the way you draw them, with words or images resting on connecting, curvy lines or 'branches', helps your memory make strong **associations**.

With Mind Maps remembering anything is a breeze, no matter how complicated. They are the **King** of Memory Tools.

Mind Maps will help you:

★ Remember who has borrowed your **CDs**
★ Take EVERYTHING you need on holiday
★ Concentrate when your mind wanders
★ Take notes in class
★ Memorize the birthdays of your mates and family
★ Research and sort information from different sources, e.g. Internet, library, museums
★ Revise for exams
★ Remember your dreams

How to Draw a Memory Mind Map

Mind Maps are really **easy** to draw as well. Let's say you've been away on a really cool holiday. Even if you've had the most **awesome** time, somehow when you're back at school they can seem a long, long way away and you start to forget what you got up to. If you draw a Mind Map of your holiday you will remember what you got up to – handy when people ask when you get back.

1. Take a sheet of plain white paper. (Don't use lined paper - it will stop your ideas flowing.) Turn the paper on to its side, 'landscape' view.

2. Take some bright felt-tip pens. Choose your favourite colours.

3. Draw a picture in the centre of the page that connects with what you did or where you went on holiday and over, under or in it write 'My Holiday' in big letters. Putting your main idea in the middle keeps you concentrating and gives you more freedom to spread out.

4. Choose a colour and draw a main branch off the central picture. Make the branch thicker where it joins on and have it getting thinner at the ends. Write your first idea about your holiday, using only one word, in **CAPITAL** letters, filling up the length of the branch. In this example Mike has just come back from a holiday abroad. His branches are '**BEACH**', '**OUTINGS**', '**HOTELS**', '**PEOPLE**' and '**ACTIVITIES**'. Add your main branches to your central image using a different colour for each one.

5. Now let your brain think of ideas to develop your main branches. If one of your main branches was 'BEACH', what did you do on it? Swim? Sunbathe? Build sand-castles? Draw thinner branches for these ideas off the main ones and write the words in small letters along them. You can also draw a little picture or symbol for each one (remember, images help your **IMAGINATION**). Simple sketches are fine – and yes, you **CAN** draw! Make sure the words and pictures touch the branches, as when they're connected on the page they'll be connected in your brain (the branches help with **ASSOCIATION**).

6. As more connected ideas come to you, add more branches to your sub-topics. You now have a complete record of your holiday – like a diary, only better! Turn over the page to see what Mike got up to on his holiday.

AMAZING BRAIN FACT
DREAM ON!
Did you know that dreaming and daydreaming **HELP** flex your imagination and so help your **MEMORY?**

TONY'S MEMORY TEASERS

1. What are the two star players of your memory?
2. What are the other players on the two teams?
3. What happens twice in a week and once in a year, but never in a day?
4. What can go up a chimney down, but can't go down a chimney up?

Answers

1. Imagination and Association.
2. Exaggeration, Laughter, Senses, Colours, Rhythm and Positive Thinking all play on the Association team. Tip: Draw a Mind Map of these two teams to help you remember all the players.
3. The letter 'e'.
4. An umbrella.

reading

sunbathing

sailing

barbecues

snorkelling

BEACH

swimming

castles

museums

castles

OUTINGS

cafés

monuments

walks

shopping

pedaloes

sunshades

loungers

dancing

My Holiday Mind Map

scuba

rock
climbing diving
          kite   flying

ACTIVITIES football
                5-a-side

PEOPLE family Mum Dad
                      Jude
                      Jim
        Juan friends
smile   guide   Kelly Dave
        taxi   Rockwood   Dido
HOTELS   Sam
        Pinas   Susie
                 pool
The Dynasty   Las
           volleyball gym

Let the Sparks Fly!

Suppose you've been set a History project at school about the Gunpowder Plot. You've searched for information in library books, on the Internet and at the local museum, making lots of notes as you went along. You now need to **sort** all the information into a logical order and remember it, so you can talk about in class. Look at the notes you might have made opposite.

How would you organize this mass of information? There is no 'right' answer as you could sort the information on your branches in lots of **different** ways, so just look for strands of information that **you** think would link well on the Mind Map branches. For example, there is a lot about religion in the notes, so that could be one of your main branches. And then there is information about the plot itself and what it involved. 'PLOT' could be another main branch.

Mind Maps encourage you to look for links (**associations**) between information and help you to sort it properly. This is why Mind Maps make it **really easy** for your brain to remember things. Even better, when you have done your Mind Map you will have all the information on **one** page (you won't have to wrestle with different sheets of paper). Wicked! Take a look at the Mind Map on p.30 to see how you could draw yours.

To learn the information for your class discussion, keep going over each of the branches in your mind. Look at the **colour** of the branch and its position on the page so you associate that colour and that location on the page with the information on it. Once you've gone over it a few times you will remember it all, no sweat.

The Gunpowder plotters tried to blow up the Houses of Parliament in 1605.

When Elizabeth I died King James VI of Scotland was her nearest living relative, so he became James I of England and also head of the Church of England.

There were three main groups of Christians in the country: the Roman Catholics, who looked to the Pope as their head; the Anglicans, who accepted the King as their head; and those who wanted to purify religion, doing away with bishops, candles, robes and ceremonies – the Puritans.

A house had been rented next to the Houses of Parliament. They were going to tunnel through to the basement and stack barrels of gunpowder under it. When King, Lords and Commons met, they would blow them up.

The idea was that the Catholics would rise up, take over the government and choose their own ruler.

James was not liked by the Catholics and a small gang of them led by Catesby and including Guido (Guy) Fawkes decided to murder him and the whole of Parliament.

One of the gang sent a warning to Lord Monteagle. The cellars were searched and Guy Fawkes was caught red-handed.

Ever since, the English have lit a bonfire on November 5th in memory of saving the Houses of Parliament. There are big fireworks displays to represent the planned gunpowder explosions. Because he was burnt to death, a dummy Guy Fawkes is burnt on top of the bonfire.

He was taken to the Tower of London and tortured to make him divulge the other plotters, but he wouldn't. He and the gang (8 in number) were sentenced to death.

27

BRAIN FLEXOR
WHAT DAY IS IT?
Can't remember what you're meant to be doing from one day to the next? No problem! Mind Map your day or your week and you'll be in the right place at the right time with everything you need.

Congratulations! You have now mastered the king of memory tools, the Mind Map. Before you get going on the next chapter, take five, have a breather – you've **earned** it!

What do you call
a cat that lives
in the desert?

Sandy Claws.

TONY'S MEMORY TEASERS

1. You enter a dark room. You have only one match. There is an oil lamp, a furnace and a stove in the room. Which would you light first?
2. A man turned out all the lights and went to bed. He woke up, saw something on the news and became very upset with himself. Why?
3. What is put on a table and cut, but never eaten?
4. What question can you ask all day long and get a different, correct answer each time?

Answers
1. The match.
2. He lived in a lighthouse. When he turned out all the lights it caused a shipwreck.
3. A deck of cards.
4. The time.

Gunpowder Plot Mind Map

MONARCHY

Elizabeth I died

James I VI

church England

Scotland

head

RELIGION

Pope

Catholics

Anglicans King

Puritans

religion

purify

PLOT

James

Lords

Commons

...rning murder

...use government replace

Catesby

Fawkes Guy

approached

...der

Repeat and Rest to Be the Best

Having a break is not just about chilling. Believe it or not, you actually learn **best** during a break!

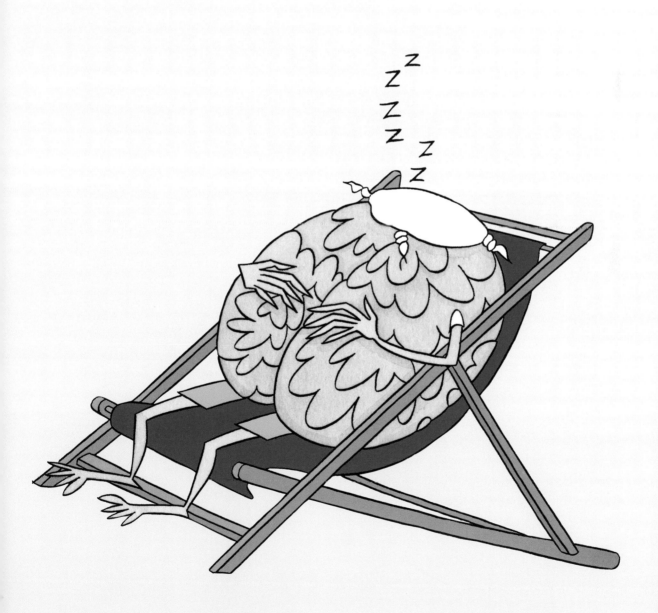

The reason why you learn best during a break is because whilst you are doing something else, your amazing brain is **busy**.

It works out what you might have found a bit tricky and solves problems for you. It then files the information away for you so it can find it quickly when you want it. Pretty cool, eh? Once it's stored that batch of information it's ready for the next lot. Your memory is always **hungry** for more; it just needs time to make room for it and store it properly.

AMAZING BRAIN FACT
RESTS FOR RESULTS

Have you ever noticed that you come up with your best ideas when you aren't trying to think of them? Where did you get that cool idea for your birthday? In the bath! Where did you crack that maths question? When you were walking home from school! It's the same for geniuses all over the world. Your brain is at its **BEST** when you give it a **REST**, so if you ever get stuck on something, get up and do something else.

Little Rests Help you Best

What sort of rests are we talking about here? At home you can be in charge of planning your own time, whether you are learning for **fun**, doing your homework or revising for exams. When you feel your brain getting a bit **weary** you can give it a little break for 5 to 10 minutes. Ideally, this should be about 45 minutes after you've started. Step outside into the fresh air, or juggle some balls (see pp38–9), or go into a different room – anything that takes your mind off what you were doing. When you come back, your brain will feel **refreshed** and will want to start learning again.

You can see this from two ropes across the River of Forgetting below. The bottom rope shows how much you can remember if you keep going for two hours without taking a break – look at how much the rope sags in the middle and at how much effort it takes to hold it up! Most things will get washed away down the River of Forgetting and snapped up by the Memory Piranhas. The kids above them are having a much easier time. They've got posts in the river to support the rope across it. Each post represents a little break. Their rope is high and dry above that pesky river – they'll remember **so** much **more!**

Become a Juggling Genius

Like to learn to juggle, but not sure how to start? It's **easy**! All you need are three small, squishy balls or bean bags that are the same size and weight – and a bit of **determination**.

Step One – With One Ball

Hold **ONE** ball in one of your hands, keeping both hands in front of you at **waist level**. With a scooping, circular movement, toss the ball up into the air in an **ARC** and into the other hand.

Keep throwing the ball backwards and forwards using this scooping motion until you can do it without thinking.

Tip: Move from your elbow to throw the ball, not just from your wrist. Stand in front of a wall until you get the hang of throwing the balls straight.

Step Two – With Two Balls

Now take **one** ball in **each** hand. First throw **ball 1** (in your **right** hand) up in an arc into your **left** hand. The **highest point** should be about eye level. When this ball reaches its highest point throw **ball 2** (in your **left** hand) up over to your **right**. Catch **ball 1** with your **left** hand and **ball 2** with your **right**. Stop!

Repeat, only this time start with your left hand instead of your right. Keep practising until you can toss the balls smoothly between both hands without hesitating.

Step Three – With Three Balls

Start with two balls, balls 1 and 3, in your best hand (in this case we'll say your right hand, but use your left if you're left-handed) and ball 2 in your left. Start by tossing **ball 1** (the **front ball** in your **right** hand) in an arc to your **left**.

When ball 1 reaches its highest point, throw **ball 2** (in your **left** hand) in an arc to your **right**. This is like Step Two.

When ball 2 reaches its highest point, toss **ball 3** from your **right** hand in an arc to your **left**. **Catch ball 2** in your **right** hand.

Tip: You'll find this bit easier if you roll ball 3 to the front of your hand before you throw it.

When ball 3 reaches its highest point throw **ball 1** (in your left hand) in an arc to your **right** hand. **Catch ball 3** in your **left** hand. Start again and keep going!

Top juggling tips:

★ Always throw the balls up in an arc
★ **Hold your hands around waist level**
★ Use different-coloured balls so you can tell them apart
★ **Toss the balls to about eye level**
★ Don't try to crack it in one session – little and often works best
★ Practise, practise, practise!

What Did You Say?

Also, have you ever noticed that you can remember more from the **beginning** of a lesson than from the middle of it? It's much easier for your mind to wander off in the middle of the class unless you are learning things that you can link together (**association!**) or if your teacher tells you something really **different** that stands out. It's only towards the end of the class that your brain starts to perk up again and you find it easier to remember stuff.

The water level of the picture to the right shows this. It starts off high, drops and rises again. The highest points of learning are the three big waves (these are the things you can link together) and the surf dude (he's what stands out). Like the ropes across the river, if you take regular breaks, there will be less information for you to learn all at once and therefore less in the 'middle zone' when it's harder to concentrate.

What did
the ocean say
to the sea?

Nothing,
it just
waved!

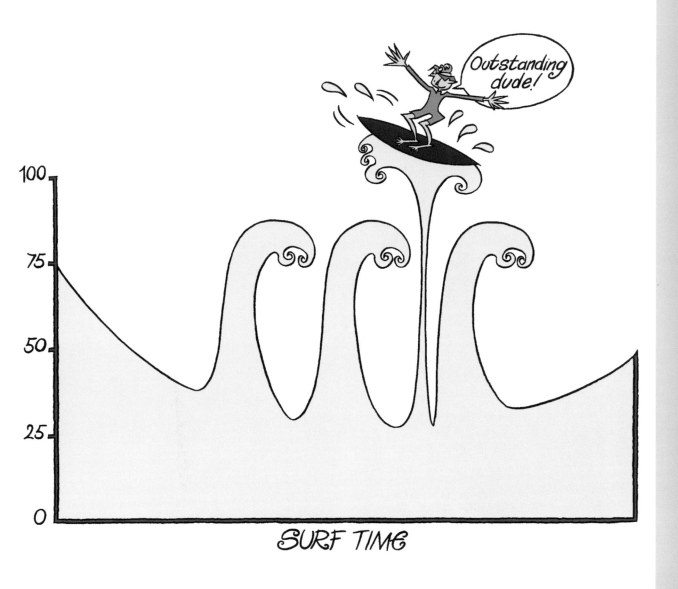

SURF TIME

AMAZING BRAIN FACT

Did you know that you have about 1 million million brain cells in that fantastic head of yours? Brain cells are so tiny that you could fit 100 of them on to a single pinhead. If you lined them all up they could reach to the moon and back. The moon is about 384,400 km (about 238,710 miles) from Earth!

Your Concentration Stallion

Chilling out is also great for your **concentration**. You need to be able to concentrate well to learn things properly. Think of your concentration as a great big **powerful** horse – a huge excitable stallion raring to go! And **you've** got to ride it! Sometimes it's easy to ride it as it wants to do what you want to do too, but sometimes it knows that your heart's not really into what you're asking it to do – let's face it, you'd rather be daydreaming about becoming a film star than how to figure out the angles of a triangle at school.

AMAZING BRAIN FACT

Did you know that different areas of your brain perform different tasks for you? The part of your brain that makes it possible for you to remember things is called the cerebrum (pronounced 'ser-ri-brum'). It's the largest part of your brain and fits like a giant shower cap over the other parts of it. This is the area of your brain that has a folded and wrinkled texture. The cerebrum is made up of two different hemispheres or sides, the left and the right. These are the two sides of the brain people mean when they refer to the left and the right brain.

Why is
orange juice
so clever?

It
concentrates!

It then goes off on mad dashes about the place, jumping over all kinds of things, which is great fun, but you do still need to know about those pesky triangles. Your concentration stallion is a **first-class** racehorse. All you need to do is learn to ride it well. Then you will be able to concentrate on the **right things** at the **right time** and cross the finishing line **miles** ahead of everybody else. How can you do that? By getting your **imagination** on board.

Imagination to the Rescue!

Sometimes it's hardest to concentrate in class because you can't take a break when you want to or need to. Try some of the following to get your **imagination** going:

★ *Draw a Mind Map of what you are being taught (see p.30). This will get your **imagination** and concentration working so your mind won't wander. It also has the added bonus of making the lesson much easier to remember. If you like, take blank 'skeleton' Mind Maps into the class with you. You can fill these in as you go along.*

★ *Look for ways to use the Memory tools in Chapter 4. For example, if you are presented with lots of dates to learn, **FIRE** up your **imagination** with the Number Shapes and Number Rhymes (see p.72 and 76); if you are reading a passage from a book that doesn't seem very exciting, start recording a Memory Movie (see p.54) to spice it up.*

★ *Look for opportunities to ask or answer questions. If you get yourself more involved in the lesson your **imagination** will work **WITH** you and the lesson will go by more quickly too.*

★ *If you think you aren't interested in a subject, use your **imagination** to link it to something that **DOES** grab your attention. For example, do you think you aren't interested in English? But don't you enjoy talking to your friends – check your phone bill (or is it your parents'?)! Well, English and chatting to your mates are actually closely **CONNECTED**. Shakespeare, the genius playwright, got his brilliant ideas from talking and listening to people. And so can you, for the stories or plays you write. So you see, if you like catching up with your mates you just have to be interested in English!*

What needs
an answer, but
doesn't ask a
question?

Your
phone!

Help! I've Got an Exam Blank

If your mind ever goes blank it is usually because you are in the spotlight and under pressure to remember. This is bad enough when your teacher asks you something in class and you can't think of anything to say, but it's a nightmare if it happens in exams. What you need to do is **relax.** Your **imagination** can get scared off when you're all tensed up – but if you chill out for a few seconds it will **always** come back to you. Let's say that you have just opened your science exam paper and need to write about gravity. You stare at the page, but you can't think of anything. Here's what to do:

★ *Close your eyes and breathe in and out SLOWLY and deeply with your hands on your tummy. Feel your belly moving in and out.*

★ *After a few seconds take a mental step back from the question and just think about the subject, gravity. Well, you KNOW that gravity is what keeps your feet on the ground.*

★ *Starting with that information, draw a quick Mind Map sketch to get your imagination moving in the RIGHT direction. You know that other planets have different gravity, as does the Moon, because you've seen clips of astronauts bouncing about on it. Add that to your Mind Map.*

★ *Keep asking yourself questions and answering them with your Mind Map. You will find that the information comes back to you and, if you drew a Mind Map about gravity as part of your revision, you will find that you start to remember the different branches of your revision Mind Map.*

TIP: if you are still struggling after a minute or two, move on to a question you **can** answer. Your memory will keep working on the tricky question and should come up with the answer when you go back to it.

Five-Times Repetition Is All it Takes

Isn't it frustrating that things you used to know **really well** and understand **perfectly** sometimes drift away from your brain, as if you never knew them in the first place? Don't panic! You're only forgetting things because you haven't reinforced them in your memory.

When you first learn something it goes into your **short-term** memory. This means that you will be able to remember it for a few minutes, a few days (or even a few weeks if you use my memory tools). If you want to remember something **for ever** you need to transfer it into your **long-term** memory. You can do this by going over what you've learnt regularly. If you keep going over information using the memory tools in this book you should only need to look at it a total of **five** times before you remember it **for good**. Think how much time, energy and worry you will save yourself when it comes to exams. So, how should you go over everything?

'Five-times repetition equals long-term memory'

First Repetition: Just after you have first learnt it

Second Repetition: One day after you first learnt it

Third Repetition: One week after you first learnt it

Fourth Repetition: One month after you first learnt it

Fifth Repetition: Three to six months after you first learnt it

After you have done the fifth repetition you will find that your **creativity** takes over. Your **imagination** will go to town with what you have already learnt and memorized, and you'll find you'll know **more**. This is because you make more and more links between everything in that amazing memory of yours. **Daydreaming** really helps here. Let your mind play around with an idea or some information and it will come alive for you.

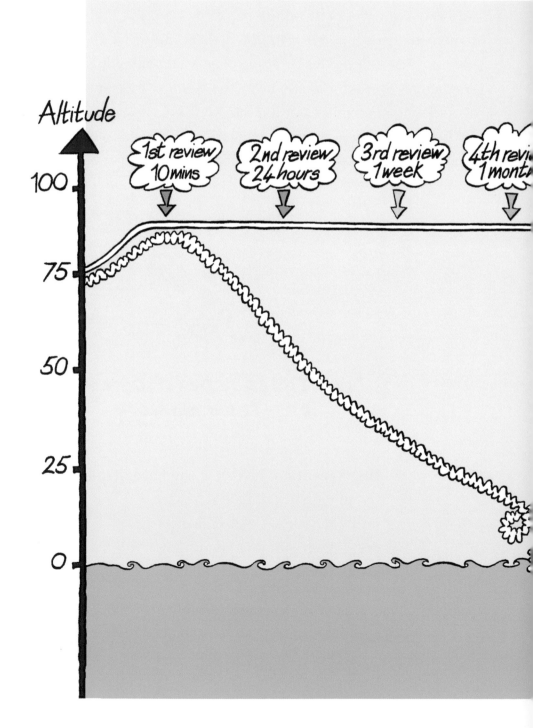

Look at the aeroplane illustration below to see the difference it makes if you go over stuff regularly. The red aeroplane shows what will happen if you don't go over things again – it goes up and then down and down because you start to lose confidence and getting things mixed up in your mind. The white aeroplane though stays high and then goes **up**. This is because you remember it all and you also start to link what you've learnt to other stuff you've learnt and you find you remember **more** and **MORE**!!

Putting Repetition into Practice

You need to be a bit organized to work out what you've gone over and when you need to go over it again. The best way to do this is to buy a large colourful calendar and get into the habit of writing down what you've learnt every day.

Spend 20 minutes going over what you did at school that day and then look back at your calendar to a week, a month and six months ago to see what else you need to go over. Make a note of anything you don't understand and ask your mates, parents or teacher about it later. If you do this you won't **ever** have a last-minute revision panic because you'll have remembered **everything** you were taught.

TONY'S MEMORY TEASERS

1. What unusual property do the words FLOUR, TERN and THIRSTY have in common?

2. The more of them you take, the more you leave behind. What are they?

3. Three men were fishing. The boat flipped over and the three men fell into the water. Two of the men got their hair wet. Why didn't the third man's hair get wet?

4. Pull one out and scratch my head. What once was red is black instead. What am I?

Answers
1. If you remove a letter from each of them, they spell a number.
2. Footsteps.
3. He was bald.
4. A match.

Memory Tips to Make it Stick

Now it's time to show you a few other top memory tools. Like Mind Maps, they work with the two star players imagination and association. You can use them on their own or with the Mind Maps you draw. These Memory tools are all about having fun with your memory, so go wild, be daring, have a laugh, be different! The more you play with your memory, the easier it is to remember EVERYTHING.

1. Memory Movies

Memory Movies are one of the **easiest** memory tools to get the hang of. All you need to do is start recording your own inner movie, making it as **colourful**, **exciting** and **exaggerated** as possible. If you really get your **imagination** involved you'll be able to remember **every** part of the action and plot. Simply imagine that you are the director of world blockbuster movies, *Harry Potter*, *Star Wars*, *Shrek* – you name it that's you! You'll need to replay your movie a few times to make sure you've included all the information you need and to properly 'set' it in your mind – remember the repetition tips in the last chapter? After that, when you need to recall the information, just press the 'play' button on your inner screen.

Memory Movies are particularly handy for memorizing:

★ How your football team scored that winning goal
★ What happened in a battle and who fought it
★ Dance moves to your favourite tune
★ How to make your favourite chocolate cake
★ What you need to do in a science experiment
★ Your Mind Maps (simply go over each branch and act out the information in your head).

AMAZING BRAIN FACT
HOW IN THE WORLD?
You have a whole universe inside your head! How? Scientists have proved that the number of thoughts that you could have is GREATER than the number of atoms in the known universe!

Where do mermaids
go to see movies?

The dive-in.

TONY'S MEMORY TEASERS

1. Jack and Jill were found gasping for breath, lying in a puddle of water with broken glass all around. What happened?

2. Only one colour, but not one size, stuck at the bottom, yet easily flies. Present in the sun, but not in the rain, doing no harm, and feeling no pain. What am I?

3. A clever thief in the olden days was charged with treason against the king and sentenced to death. But the king decided to be a little lenient so he let the thief choose his own way to die. What way should the thief choose?

4. Where can you stand up straight, but still be considered sideways?

Answers

1. Jack and Jill were goldfish and their bowl had been knocked over.
2. A shadow.
3. To die of old age.
4. The equator. You would be standing up straight in relation to the ground, but you'd be standing sideways in relation to the Earth's axis.

Lights, Camera, Action!

Think about the planets. Can you name them all in the right order? Do you know which ones are **big**, **small** or little? (Tip: there are 4 little, 4 big and 1 small planet.) With a Memory Movie you'll remember if they are big or small planets; you'll remember them in order. **For ever!**

Here's a list of the planets in the correct order from the Sun:

1. Mercury
2. Venus
3. Earth
4. Mars
5. Jupiter
6. Saturn
7. Uranus
8. Neptune
9. Pluto

If you just try to remember them as a list it would be a real sweat. Instead get your **imagination** whirring with a Memory Movie.

What do you get
if you cross a
centipede with
a parrot?

A
walkie-talkie!

... AAAAnd ACTION!

Imagine the SUN. It's a beautiful glowing red-orange ball of heat. Feel the heat; smell the heat. Next to the Sun imagine a small thermometer filled with the shiny liquid metal that measures temperatures called … MERCURY!

Watch the mercury rising to the top as the Sun gets hotter and hotter, until it **explodes**, and all the little balls of mercury (little because Mercury is a small planet) drop to the ground.

Next, imagine a small – again it's a small planet – but beautiful goddess, glowing brilliantly in the light of the Sun. Imagine what she is wearing; smell her perfume. It's **VENUS**, the planet of love. Watch as she picks up a tiny silver ball of mercury and throws it with awesome power up into the sky until it comes hurtling down to land with a giant **thump** in your garden. And what planet would that be? **EARTH**!

The ball of mercury sends clods of earth into your next-door neighbour's garden. This really winds him up. He comes rushing out, a small – yes, he is a small planet – red-faced and very angry character holding a chocolate bar. It's **MARS**, the red planet of war.

Suddenly, striding down the street, comes a giant over 200 metres tall with a big 'J'-shaped lock of hair falling over his eyes. He is the king of the gods and the biggest planet: **JUPITER**. Jupiter tells Mars to get back in his house and stop ranting. You look up at Jupiter and on his giant chest in enormous letters is the word 'SUN'. Each of these large letters stands for the first letter of the next three big planets (although they're not as big as giant Jupiter): 'S' for **SATURN**, 'U' for **URANUS** and 'N' for **NEPTUNE**. Next you see, sitting on Jupiter's head, a little – because it's a really little planet – dog, it's a dalmation who goes by the name of … **PLUTO**! **CUT!**

Now play back the movie. RE-VIEW it. RE-VISION it. Really get all your **senses** involved. The visual memories you have of the story will enable the list of planets to come bouncing back into your mind and all in the right order, too.

Did you remember them all? Yes? **awesome**! Not quite? All you need to do is make the images **stronger** in your mind.

Go back to your movie and rerecord the bit you're not sure of – really get your **imagination** on board to make the image stronger. Use **all** your senses and hey presto! You'll find that your brain will remember it. For example, if you weren't sure about Venus imagine the beautiful goddess all over again. She might have golden hair that drifts out behind her. Think about what she is wearing. She could be wearing a floaty, long white dress that has specks of shiny mercury on it from the thermometer **exploding**.

BRAIN BLANKS

If you ever forget something in an exam, stay calm. Simply take your mind back to where you were when you learnt it. Were you sitting at your desk at school? Or were you sitting in your bedroom revising? Which book was it in? Where was it on the page? Your mind so loves location that it is very likely that you will jog your memory and remember it. (For more tips on remembering things under pressure see p.46.)

Mini-Memory Tools

Acronyms – Acro-what? Think of acrobatics with words! – are another handy way of remembering information. It's pronounced 'ak-row-nim'. All you do is take the first letter of each word you want to learn and make them spell another word. **Easy**!

Say you want to learn the names of the five Great Lakes in North America. These are **Huron, Ontario, Michigan, Erie and Superior**. If you put together the first letter of each of these names they spell the word **homes**. To link the word 'homes' with the lakes you would only have to record a Mini-Memory Movie of the houses on your street floating on a huge lake. When it comes to remembering the names of the lakes, you will remember all the homes floating on water and that each lake begins with one of the letters in **homes**. Easy!

Six Ladies, One Man

Now create your own movie for remembering the order of Henry VIII's six wives and what happened to them:

Catherine of Aragon – Divorced
Anne Boleyn – Beheaded
Jane Seymour – Died
Anne of Cleves – Divorced
Catherine Howard – Beheaded
Catherine Parr – Survived

You can set up your movie any way you want. Have a go before you read the suggestions below. Remember, there is no one 'correct' script for your Memory Movie – it's all about what captures **your imagination** so you can remember the action.

Ideas to Help You Record Your Memory Movies

If you know something about each wife, for example that Catherine of Aragon was from Spain, you can use that information to record your movie. In this case you might imagine a sad Catherine of Aragon sailing down the Thames on a stately Spanish galleon, with Anne Boleyn on the bank holding her severed head high in the air so she can see over the people in front of her. If you don't know much about them, you could play with their names, for example, Jane Seymour who died was 'Se-en no more'.

How about Anne of Cleves? What do you know about her? Well, she was famous for being incredibly ugly and Henry VIII had to pay her a **huge** amount of money when he divorced her. How about imagining a very ugly lady dressed in expensive clothes sitting comfortably on an enormous pile of gold coins?

And what about the two Catherines, Catherine Howard and Catherine Parr? Let's say you don't know very much about them either apart from knowing that one was beheaded and one died. For Catherine Howard you could play on her surname by thinking 'How [h]ard' Henry was on her for chopping off her head. For Catherine Parr you could remember her name because she 'Parr-tied' on without Henry after he died – and imagine her dancing about having fun!

AMAZING BRAIN FACT
CHAMPION OF THE WORLD!
At the 2004 World Memory Championships 12-year-old Lara Hick from Germany memorized the order of an entire pack of 52 shuffled cards in a staggering 2 minutes 24 seconds. She set a new kids', world record!

Mini-Memory Tools

Rhyme, word plays and song are excellent mini-memory tools to help you remember things that seem to be a bit dreary, like lists of words or grammar rules. They are also a great excuse to have **fun** with your memory – and the more fun you have learning something the more likely you are to remember it.

★ **Rhyme.** *Making up little rhymes can help fix facts in your memory, such as the famous: 'In 1666 London burnt like rotten sticks' or 'In 1492 Columbus sailed the ocean blue'.*

★ **Word plays.** *If you need to remember an unfamiliar name or a word in a foreign language, try to look for a way to **play** on the word. For example, say you are finding it tricky remembering in French that 'sur' means 'on' but 'sous' means 'under'. You could remember 'sur' as being on the 'surface' and 'sous' standing for '**so**mewhere **u**nder the surface'.*

★ **Song.** *Ever wondered why it's so easy to remember the words to your fave song but much harder to remember dates, names or tricky facts? A good song has rhythm, catchy lyrics and you **enjoy** listening to it and want to sing along too. Make facts that don't grab you more exciting by putting them to music you like or know well. For example, if you need to know the Roman system for numbering things (Roman numerals) you could set the traditional rhyme below to the tune you used for learning the alphabet when you were little, your 'ABC':*

'X' shall stand for playmates ten,

'V' for five stout stalwart men,

'I' for one as I'm alive,

'C' for a hundred, 'D' for five*,

'M' for a thousand soldiers true,

And 'L' for fifty I'll tell you!

*D stands for five *hundred*

2. Tony's Memory Palace

Have you ever gone to do something but got distracted on the way and completely forgotten what you originally thought of? It's only when you go back to where you were that you remember. Why is this? It's because your brain is good at remembering where things are, where they are **located**.

You can use your mind's liking for location with my Memory Palace. I got this idea from the Romans – they were great inventors and they invented this memory technique. They called it the Room System. I prefer to call it the palace, as it is a fantastic p(a)lace to put lots of things in your mind. The key to the Memory Palace is to keep it and **all** the things inside it in the **same** place. This means that you can place what you want to **remember** on what is **already in there**. It's a bit like the wardrobe we talked about on p.16. You 'hang' the information on something you already know. The Memory Palace works so well because it uses **association** to **link** information

Why don't anteaters get sick?

Because they are full of ant(i)bodies!

TONY'S MEMORY TEASERS

1. What's the order of the planets from the Sun? Replay that Memory Movie of yours!
2. A man was asked what his daughters looked like. He answered, 'They are all blondes, but two, all brunettes, but two, and all redheads, but two.' How many daughters did he have?
3. It cannot be seen, cannot be felt, cannot be heard, cannot be smelt. It lies behind stars and under hills and empty holes it fills. What is it?
4. Six glasses are in a row. The first three are full of juice; the second three are empty. By moving only one glass, can you arrange them so empty and full glasses alternate?

Answers
1. Mercury, Venus, Earth, Mars, Jupiter, Saturn, Uranus, Neptune, Pluto.
2. Three: one blond, one brunette and one redhead.
3. Darkness.
4. Pour the juice from the second glass into the fifth.

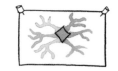

A P(a)lace in your Memory

First of all you need to use that **imagination** of yours to kit out your memory palace. Take a bit of time to do this and draw a Mind Map to help you so you know what each room contains and in what order you see it.

So, what's the first thing you see when you enter your palace? Let's say it's a great big white shiny **marble staircase** stretching up and up to the first floor. Add that to your Mind Map. Then what? What else can you see as you look up? A glittering **chandelier** hanging from the ceiling tinkling as it moves? OK, add that too. What are you standing on? A bright blue **rug** with long yellow tassels? You wiggle your toes into it and feel how soft it is. Anything else in the great hallway? A big old **grandfather clock** ticking away in the corner? When you've got the main things in the hall, go into the next room. What is it? The sitting room? Look around, what's the first thing you see? A beautiful **fish tank** filled with bright red fish swimming back and forth?

Really use your **imagination** and senses until you have a very **clear picture** of it all in your mind.

Remember, you'll need to go over your Mind Map a few times to set it in your memory. Your Mind Map will be your **record** of all the things in your palace that you can hang things on. If you like, use your own house as your memory palace.

The Palace in Action

Supposing you need to remember the following list of things:

- ⭐ *to take the dog for a walk*
- ⭐ *a Playstation*
- ⭐ *a football*
- ⭐ *your camera*
- ⭐ *your packed lunch*
- ⭐ *your mobile*
- ⭐ *your geography project*
- ⭐ *to clean your fish tank*
- ⭐ *your latest CD*
- ⭐ *flowers for your Mum*

Right, have you got that Memory Palace of yours clear in your mind? Wicked! Remember, let your imagination run wild! OK, the first thing you need to memorize is to **walk the dog**. Imagine your dog running up and down the great **marble staircase**. Hear his excited whimpers, the bash of his wagging tail and the click-clack of his paws as he scrabbles up and down the stairs with his lead in his mouth.

What's the next thing in your house? The **chandelier**? And what do you need to remember? Ah yes! The **Playstation**. How could you link the Playstation with the chandelier? How about the Playstation coming to life, jumping onto the chandelier like a cat and landing on it with a loud tinkling? Watch the chandelier and the cable of the Playstation swing back and forth.

The next thing you need to remember is the **football**. What's it like? Let's say it's a gleaming white, smooth leather football. Smell that leather! Bounce the football up and down on the bright blue rug a couple of times then wrap the **rug** around it like a giant soft sweetie wrapper.

How are we doing? What's next in your palace? A **grandfather clock**? Now you need to remember the camera. Open up the clock and hang the **camera** from its pendulum. Watch it sway back and forth and hear the tick of the clock and the clunk of the camera as it hits the sides of the clock case.

Over to you!

Now it's your turn! Keep going with the remaining six things you need to remember and use your **imagination** to link them to the next object in your palace. Do **whatever** you want to the objects to create an **association**.

3. Numbers and Shapes to Remember in Haste

The next two memory tools, the Number–Shape and the Number–Rhyme tools, use numbers. The idea is that you use the numbers like **anchors** for what you need to remember – a bit like how you link what you want to remember to things in your Memory Palace. Like the Memory Palace, when you want to remember the information, all you need to do is to think about how you **linked** it with the numbers. Then you'll remember it **all**, *no problemo!* Let's start with the numbers and shapes. Like all the other memory tools, this one works so well because it uses **imagination** and **association**, the two star players of memory.

It's the Shape that Counts

Take a look at the numbers opposite and the images beside them. Can you see how each image is shaped like the actual number? Spend some time studying them and learning which image goes with which number. Draw a **Mind Map** with a main branch for each number. On the main branch write down the number and on the sub-branch draw the image. Keep going over your Mind Map so that you link each **number** with its **image**.

Next practise the numbers and their shapes. What is your phone number? Write it down using your number–shapes. What about your date of birth? Use the shapes to write that down, too. When you've got the hang of the number–shapes, you can use them to **all** sorts of things, especially:

★ *Lists of things in order*
★ *Birthdays, dates you did things or for history*
★ *Phone numbers – great if you forget your mobile!*
★ *Times of things, e.g. a good film on TV, start of a match, lessons*

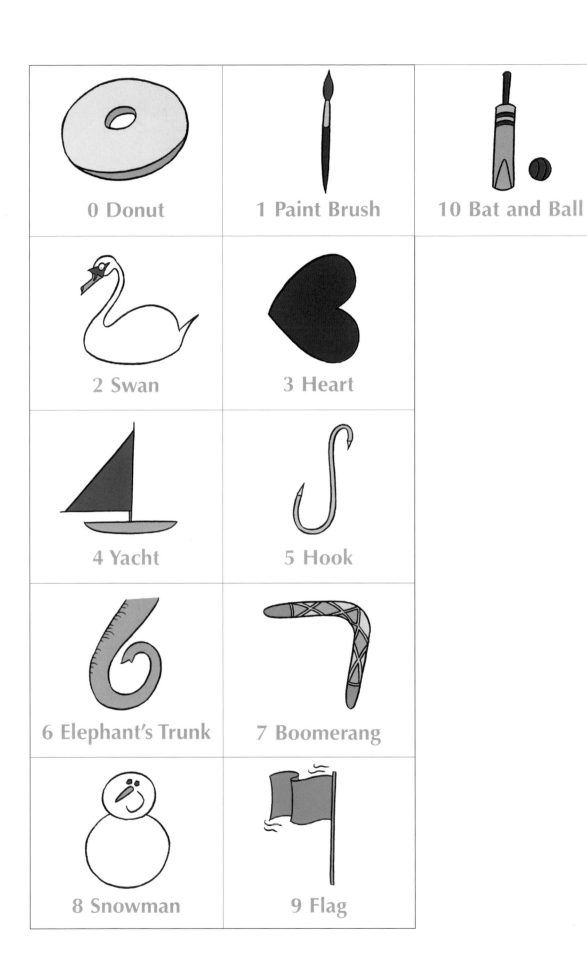

0 Donut

1 Paint Brush

10 Bat and Ball

2 Swan

3 Heart

4 Yacht

5 Hook

6 Elephant's Trunk

7 Boomerang

8 Snowman

9 Flag

Now it's time for you to have some **fun** with numbers. Let's say you want to remember the following list of things in order:

0	**Feed goldfish**
1	Skateboard
2	Pizza
3	Baseball cap
4	**Key**
5	**CD**
6	Backpack
7	Football boots
8	**Homework**
9	Present for Gran
10	**Bath**

All you need to do is to **rev up** that Formula One **imagination** of yours and dream up a scenario to link the item with the number. You'll be **amazed** at how easy it is to remember them **all** in order! So, how could you link the items on the list with these number images?

0   **For feeding the goldfish**, you might imagine throwing hundreds of **doughnuts** into a gigantic fish tank and the fish splashing around in a frenzy to gobble them up.

1   For skateboard you could imagine your friend Dan coming racing down the hill on his skateboard waving a gigantic **paintbrush** and spattering colourful paints all over the place.

2   For pizza you can think of a whole flock of beautiful white **swans** pecking at a huge pizza they have found floating down the river.

3   For baseball cap you could imagine a bright red baseball cap with an enormous **heart**-shaped peak jutting out the front.

4   **For key** you might imagine that you are on your beautiful sparkling new **yacht**. You throw out the anchor, but it's not an anchor, it's a great big golden key.

5   **For CD** you could imagine throwing a shiny CD up in the air to land with a rattle on a smooth metal **hook**.

6 **For backpack** you can think of an elephant strolling down your local high street with your backpack held in his **trunk** – trumpeting triumphantly as he goes.

7 **For football boots** you could imagine throwing a colourful **boomerang** and it coming back to you with your muddy wet football boots dangling on either side!

8 **For homework** you might imagine building a gigantic **snowman** in your back garden, complete with coals for eyes and a carrot for a nose and then getting him to do your homework for you.

9 **For Gran's present** you might imagine your Gran sticking a **flag** on its flag pole into a great big shiny present and the flag flapping loudly in the wind.

10 **For bath** you could imagine hitting the **ball** with your **bat** into a hot bubbly bath. The ball lands with a great splash in the water and covers you with warm, sweet-smelling, soapy bubbles.

Again, you will need to go over these scenarios a few times before you can remember them permanently.

4. It Takes No Time with Numbers and Rhyme

This number tool is similar to how you use numbers and shapes, but instead of linking the **numbers** to a **shape** you link them to a word that **rhymes** with them. You can use it to learn the same sort of things. Look at the numbers below. Say the number and its rhyming word out loud to yourself.

0 Hero	5 Hive	10 Hen
1 Bun	6 Sticks	
2 Shoe	7 Heaven	
3 Tree	8 Skate	
4 Door	9 Vine	

Like you did for the Number–Shapes, go through them several times and draw a simple **Mind Map** to help you remember them. Without looking back, which word rhymes with **4**? **Door**! Which word rhymes with **8**? **Skate**! You see! It's easy!

Practise the numbers with numbers you know (like your phone number) by saying the rhyming words; for example, Hero, Shoe, Hero, Skate, Sticks, Skate, Sticks, Door, Hive, Shoe, Tree for 020 8686 4523.

What falls
but never
breaks?

Night.

AMAZING BRAIN FACT
SOMETHING'S FISHY ABOUT OUR FACTS
Heard all the jokes about goldfish and their three-second memories? Well, it turns out we've been underestimating our scaly friends. Scientists at Plymouth University, Great Britain, have shown that goldfish have a memory span of up to three months and can even tell the time. The team of researchers trained fish to collect food at particular times of day and even trained them to press levers to release it into their tanks.

When you've got the hang of the Number–Rhymes, see if you can use them to remember this list of objects:

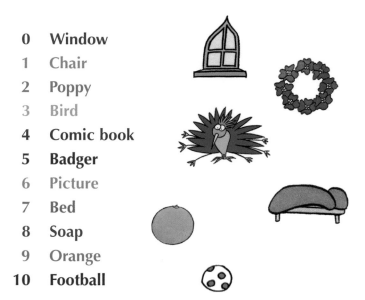

0	**Window**
1	Chair
2	**Poppy**
3	Bird
4	**Comic book**
5	**Badger**
6	Picture
7	Bed
8	**Soap**
9	Orange
10	**Football**

To remember these things all you have to do is **link** them with your word rhymes in the **strongest** way you can. You've guessed it! It's all about **imagination** and **association**. Look at the example opposite to see how you could do this.

What did the
window say to
the door?

What are you
squeaking about?
I'm the one with
the pane!

0 Hero/window

Imagine an action **hero**, muscles bulging, fists clenched and teeth gleaming, crashing through a **window** to help you fight off your enemies. Hear the sound of the glass shattering and the battle cry of your hero smashing in to save the day.

You have now connected the **hero** with **window** by conjuring up a strong image of the hero smashing through the window, using your senses to fix it in your mind. And because you know that hero rhymes with zero you will know that zero goes with window! Easy or what?

Let's have a look at the other numbers and how you could link them to objects.

1 Bun/chair

Imagine a HUGE **bun** sitting on a very flimsy **chair**. The bun is so heavy that legs are starting to collapse! Smell the freshly cooked cakey smell. Taste your favourite, delicious bun!

2 Shoe/poppy

Imagine your favourite **shoe** (a trainer maybe?) with a bright red **poppy** growing out of it. You want to pick it but the stalk is very hairy and tickles your fingers.

3 Tree/bird

Imagine a tall **tree** with a beautiful yellow **bird** sitting in it. It's singing the happiest song you've ever heard. You dance under the tree to the beat of its song – you feel on top of the world!

4 Door/comic book

Imagine your bedroom **door** is made from the brightly coloured pages of your favourite comic book. Look at all the different characters running across the pages. Hear the paper rustle as you open your door.

5 Hive/badger

Imagine a **badger** sniffing at a **beehive**. Instead of being black  and white stripped it's yellow and black stripped like a bee. See the honey oozing down its fur on to its paws. Reach out with your finger to taste a sweet gooey drop.

6 Sticks/picture

Imagine using four smooth and polished **sticks** to frame your favourite **picture** of you and your family.

7 Heaven/bed

Imagine all the angels in **heaven** sleeping peacefully on a big, white, soft **bed**.

8 Skate/soap

Imagine yourself skating but instead of **skates** you have two large bars of bright pink **soap** strapped to your feet! As you zoom around you leave trails of soapsuds behind you.

9 Vine/orange

Imagine a gigantic curly **vine**, just like the one Jack climbed in Jack and the Beanstalk. Instead of grapes, there are juicy **oranges** hanging on the vine.

10 Hen/football

Imagine a **hen** on a nest but instead of an egg it has just laid a black and white **football**.

With a little practice, it will be possible for you to remember eleven out of eleven **associations each time**. You will soon see that you can use this system for different purposes. For example, if you want to remember numbers you just memorize the rhyming words: bun, shoe, tree equals one, two, three! Your brain finds it **far** easier to remember the rhyming images than the numbers alone.

DOUBLE YOUR NUMBERS!

You can use the two number techniques together to remember **DOUBLE** the amount of information. Let's say you have two separate lists of words to remember. You can remember one list with the Number–Shape technique and the other with the Number–Rhyme.

Blue Peter Magic

Did you see me on the BBC programme *Blue Peter* in 2004? I was given a dartboard to look at. Hidden behind each number was a picture of something connected to *Blue Peter*. They gave me a few minutes to memorize this then covered up all the pictures. At the end of the programme they tested me to see if I could still remember it all. Scary? No! I had great fun! I used the Number–Shape tool to remember them all – and remember them I did. And so now could you!

BRAIN FLEXOR

When you get up tomorrow morning, write down a list of five words and give yourself one minute to remember them in the right order, using one of the number techniques. Put the piece of paper in your pocket and think about something else.

At lunchtime, think about the words again. Can you remember them? (If not, go over them again, making stronger associations between numbers and the words.) Put the paper back in your pocket and test yourself again before dinner. Can you still remember them? **Fantastic**! Next time, try to remember 10 words in a minute, then 20 ...

Congratulations! You've now learnt five **master memory tools**: Mind Maps, Memory Movies, Memory Palace and the two number techniques. You'll need to keep practising them so that they become **second nature**. This way you'll be able to memorize anything you want quickly. Now it's time to put all the memory tools together and **flex** that memory muscle of yours!

Why was the little bird expelled from school?

She was always playing practical yolks.

Flex Your Memory Muscle

5

Whatever you want to memorize, however simple or complicated, the memory tools in this book will make it possible. What? Anything? Yes, anything – remember, you only use less than 1 per cent of your brain's space for remembering things.

The more you learn and use your memory, the **fitter** your memory gets and the **easier** it is to remember more. So, whether it's the details of 100 remarkable people in history or your friends' birthdays you can remember it. Let's have a look at the kinds of things you might want to remember.

Don't Sweat the Small Stuff

Every day there are lots of information bites that you need to be able to **remember**. They're only little things, but somehow they seem so easy to forget. What sort of things are we thinking of?

★ *The name of the new boy or girl in your class*
★ *Match scores*
★ *List of things, like what to take with you on holiday or a shopping list*
★ *Phone numbers*
★ *Things you have to take with you, like your P.E. kit*
★ *Grammar rules for English or foreign languages*

Well, with your memory tools you won't forget them. You'll find the number techniques, Memory Movies and Memory Palace are the **best tools** for remembering them quickly. Flex that memory of yours and set it to remembering some of these **now**.

Play with your Memory

There are **loads** of fantastic games that will really flex your memory muscle – the ones in this book like Kim's Game, Pairs and Auntie Sal only scrape the surface of games smart people have invented. Chess, for example, has been the favourite game of the cleverest geniuses in the world and is a brilliant memory builder. Chewing over word searches, crosswords and spot-the-difference puzzles is also **great** for flexing your memory.

TONY'S MEMORY TEASERS

1. How many times do you need to go over
   something before you can remember it for ever?
2. How long should you leave between each review?
3. How does taking breaks help your memory?
   Tip: Think of the rope across a river.
4. How often should you take a break and how long
   should your breaks last?

Answers
1. Five times.
2. First review: about 10 minutes; second review: 24 hours; third review:
    1 week; fourth review: 6 months.
3. It makes the middle of your learning period shorter – the time when it's
    hardest to concentrate.
4. You should take a 5 or 10 minute break about every 45 minutes.

Game for a Name

The best way to remember a person's name is to get that **imagination** of yours going. **Play** with his or her name, use something about their appearance, anything you like. Do you know someone with the same name? Record a mini-Memory Movie of them hanging out together. You can also help yourself remember their name, by repeating it out loud when they first tell you.

How could you remember these names?

★　*Rosie – the shy new girl in your class*

★　*Raphael – your friend's cousin visiting from Mexico City*

★　*Harry – your brother's new whacky friend*

★　*Mrs Stobbart – a new teacher at school*

★　*Dave and Mel – friends of your parents*

For **Rosie** you could imagine a beautiful pink **rose** peeping around the door of your classroom. For **Gabriel** you could imagine him as an **angel** (Gabriel is the name of a famous angel) flying from Mexico City to where you are.

What about the others? Over to you!

What do you
call a mosquito
with a tin suit?

A bite in
shining armour.

AMAZING BRAIN FACT
HAVE WE MET BEFORE?
Aged 12, Katharina Bunk from Germany was a Junior World Memory Champion. In November 2003 she remembered the names and faces of 90 people in just 15 minutes.

Score Wars

If it's been an **exciting** match the chances are you will still remember the score a few days later, but what about a few **weeks** later when you are comparing notes with your mates about how your team has played all season?

There are a few ways you could remember the scores. The **number tools** come in handy here. A **Mind Map** would also be good as you could keep **adding** all the scores to it.

Imagine these are scores from a World Cup that you want to remember:

Brazil 2 – Spain 1

Ireland 1 – Russia 1

England 3 – Germany 2

China 2 – Russia 1

Use one of the number tools to link the scores with each match and country and then draw a **Mind Map**. Here's how you could remember the first two scores with the **Number–Rhyme** tool:

For the Brazil–Spain match, the score was 2 (shoe) 1 (bun) to Brazil. For this you could imagine a big yellow (the Brazilian team wear yellow) football **shoe** kicking a massive **bun** shaped like the map of Spain. Can you can see bits of bread flying all over the place with each kick?

For Ireland and Russia the score was 1 (bun) 1 (bun). Imagine two big **buns** head to head trying to push each other away. One of the buns is bright **green** and has a great big Shamrock sticking out the top (a Shamrock is the national symbol of Ireland) while the other one is bright **purple** and shaped like a beetroot – beetroot soup is a national favourite in Russia.

Now over to you!

Don't Resist the Fun of a List!

You can make a **game** of remembering lists of things in order with your friends and family – for example when you're on a long journey. If it's a long list, the best memory tools for this are **Memory Movies** and your **Memory Palace**.

Let's start with Memory Movies. Imagine your auntie is going on a very long trip. She is trying to decide what to put in her backpack and you are going to help her. Each one of you takes it in turn to choose something she will need to take, but before she can pack it you have to **remember** what she's already put in there. Record a Memory Movie as you go along to remember all the items she takes with her. Imagine these are the items that have been suggested so far:

1. **Insect repellent**
2. Sunhat
3. Flip-flops
4. **Swimming costume**
5. **Beach towel**
6. **A good book**
7. Pyjamas
8. Toothbrush

You could record your Memory Movie a bit like this:

Auntie Sal is off to Outer Mongolia

Imagine yourself walking through a jungle. Suddenly you are attacked by an enormous cloud of buzzing mosquitoes – you can hear that high-pitched buzzing sound all around you. Where is that **insect repellent**? Quick! Spray it on! A bit further on, you come to a sunny clearing – you can feel the hot sun beating down on the back of your neck. You jam your **sunhat** quickly on to your head. Then you suddenly realize that your walking boots are rubbing your little toes. Ouch! On inspection – you discover a couple of pesky blisters. But who cares? You put on your **flip-flops** instead! You are feeling a bit hot and sweaty by now, but help is at hand. A delightful waterfall is splashing into a cool, blue rock pool. You quickly change into your **swimming costume** and plunge in. The cold water feels amazing and you start swimming. Refreshed, you clamber out and dry off with your **beach towel**, which feels wonderfully soft against your skin. You feel reinvigorated and rest for a while to read your **good book**. When you arrive back at your camp, you suddenly feel very sleepy and start to yawn and stretch. Time for bed! You change into your **pyjamas**, grab your **toothbrush** and head for the bathroom.

Pack Up and Go with Your Memory Palace

How about using your **Memory Palace** (see p.66) to remember everything for auntie Sal's trip? Have you got a **clear** picture of your Memory Palace in your head? Great! If not, take a quick look at the Mind Map you made of it to refresh your memory.

Now look at the first word on the list below of what's been chosen so far and use your imagination to link it to the first item in your Memory Palace. Keep going until you've put all the items on the list in your Memory Palace.

1. **Flippers**
2. CD player
3. **Suntan lotion**
4. **Joke book**
5. **Camera**
6. **Beach towel**
7. **Shampoo**
8. Sketch pad
9. **Batteries**
10. **Hair-clip**

AMAZING BRAIN FACT

Did you know that migratory birds have excellent long-term memories? Every year around 50 billion birds fly back to the same sites to breed or spend the winter. Some, like the Arctic tern, fly an incredible 10,000 kilometres (6,214 miles) or more. To find their way back they set their internal compasses to the sun, moon or stars. They are also guided by the earth's magnetic field. Some even rely on their finely tuned sense of smell to reach their destinations.

Here's how you could remember the first thing on your shopping list to get you started:

Flippers. Imagine you are wearing your **flippers** and are running up and down the great white marble **staircase** in your Memory Palace. Hear the thwack, thwack of the rubber slapping each step.

CD player. Imagine that your **chandelier** has lots of **CDs** hanging from it instead of the crystals. Watch how the CDs reflect the light as they move against each other.

Now it's your turn!

What did the
leg bone say to
the foot?

Stick with
me and you'll
go places.

It Seems Big, But Your Memory Is Bigger

It's all very well remembering the small bits of information, but what about things that are more complicated? Things like:

- ★ *Lines for a big **role** in a play*
- ★ *Role plays for foreign **languages***
- ★ *Plot and characters in a **book** you're studying*
- ★ *What you've **dreamt** the night before*
- ★ *The **kings** and **queens** of England*
- ★ *Complicated processes in **science** or **geography***
- ★ *A **dance routine** to your favourite tune*
- ★ *The rules of a game or **sport***
- ★ *The ages and **birthdays** of everybody in your class at school*

This is where the King of Memory tools, the Mind Map, really comes into its own – and often in combination with the number tools and Memory Movies. Get that memory of yours moving and working on some of these now.

AMAZING BRAIN FACT

★ In 2004 16-year-old Joachim Thaler from Austria memorized 44 history dates chosen for him at random in an amazing 5 minutes. This is about the same number of dates that the average history student has to learn in a **YEAR**!! Impressive or what?

TONY'S MEMORY TEASER

Deep in the Outer Mongolian jungle, auntie Sal woke one morning and felt something in the pocket of her pajamas. It had a head and a tail, but no legs. When auntie Sal got up she could feel it move inside her pocket. It didn't freak her out though and she simply went about preparing her breakfast. Why on earth wasn't she concerned?

She knew it was only a coin.

Answer

The Ages and Birthdays of Everybody in Your Class

Let's say you have 20 people in your class and that whenever one of you has a birthday you all celebrate it together with a big **cake** and **candles**. As form captain you have to organize a cake on each person's **big** day, which also means that you need to remember when everybody's birthday is. How can you remember them all? **Easy!** With a **Mind Map** of course.

You could draw your Mind Map in a number of ways. You could have 12 branches for each **month** of the year and add sub-branches of the people who have birthdays in that month. Or you could do it **alphabetically** by your friends' names. Either way, you will find it really **easy** to remember when everybody's birthday is and how old each person will be.

Imagine the list below is of the people in your class. Draw a Mind Map so you can remember their birthdays. You could, of course, ask everybody in your class for their dates and draw a Mind Map with their actual birthdays and ages on it.

1. **Anjum, 22nd February**
2. Anna, 3rd June
3. Ben, 27th May
4. Charlie, 3rd June
5. **Dave, 4th November**
6. **Ellie, 30th November**
7. **Felix, 3rd December**
8. George, 13th March
9. Hamish, 5th September
10. Iris, 23rd October
11. **Karen, 4th January**
12. **Milly, 3rd July**
13. **Noah, 19th August**
14. Olivia, 16th January

15. Olja, 1st November
16. Paulo, 8th March
17. Ricky, 17th June
18. **Stacey, 24th September**
19. **Tom, 24th December**
20. Violet, 25th April

BRAIN FLEXOR
PAIRS

Have you ever tried this one? Lay out a pack of cards, face down, on the floor. Each person takes it in turns to turn over two cards at a time, and then turn them back again. The idea is to collect as many pairs as possible. The person who has collected the most pairs wins.

Quickly number the cards along the bottom row and up the left-hand side – rather like on a map. Use only one of the number systems for this as you'll need the other system to remember the number of the card. Every time you turn over a card work out the 'grid' reference number, say 3 across and 4 up. You can then quickly use your imagination to link the numbers 3 and 4 with the number and image of the suit on the card.

Class Birthdays Mind Map

Lines for a Big Role in a Play

When you want to remember lines for a play think of your play as a **Memory Movie**. All you need to do is to record your role in your head in an extremely **colourful** way. Really get all your **senses** involved. Let's say you are playing the role of a brave captain and that a pirate ship has just come to shore. Standing by a window your lines are:

'Thunder and lightening! Pirate Boreas is here. Quick, quick – to the castle walls! Arms at the ready! You there! Where's my sword?'

Really imagine how you would be feeling. How would you say your lines? Would you be **excited**? Afraid? **Pleased**? Would you be standing still? What would you be doing with your hands? Really make the lines come **alive** in your mind. If you do this, you will remember **all** your lines and, **even better**, act them out like a real Hollywood **star**! To help you even more, draw a **Mind Map** of the key parts of the action and add little images of what you will be doing on stage on the same branches as your key words.

If you haven't already got lines to learn, have a go with some or all of this speech below. Start by recording a **Memory Movie** of what you will be doing, saying and feeling. Then draw a **Mind Map** to sum it all up. The Mind Map overleaf shows you how you could Mind Map it.

Captain Boldheart
[on castle tower]:

'Thunder and lightning! Pirate Boreas is here.
Quick, quick – to the castle walls! Arms at
the ready! You there! Where's my sword?
[Page brings sword.]

Ah, yes. That's the one. Noble sword! Made of
Spanish steel by my father's hand.
[Holds the sword up.]

Fight with me today and bring me to my enemy.
Let me avenge my dear brother – murdered by
wicked Boreas.
*[Walks to centre of room and starts
to act out memory.]*

Pirate Boreas crept in at night to steal my
three fair sisters. My noble brother heard the
noise and in he ran. Sword in hand he
challenged Boreas.
[Holds up sword in challenge.]

But Boreas tricked my brother. He said he
would surrender and my poor brother, believing
him, went to show him out. Boreas saw his
chance and thrust his sword deep into my
brother's heart. My brother could not live and
Boreas escaped. But no!
[Returns to tower window.]

I shall not weep, I shall not rest, until my
sword has met his heart. Boreas you'll meet
your end, for Captain Boldheart wants revenge!
[Exits.]

Captain Boldheart Mind Map

brother

tricked heart sword thrust

died

escape

REVENGE

window tower

weep not

rest

sword

heart his met

THUNDER lightning

Boreas

pirate

tain
heart

CASTLE

walls

arms

ready

Placing People in History

The thing about history is that you learn about lots of different people and events but you don't always know how they all relate to each other. **Mind Maps** are the **perfect** tool to get you clued up about who fitted in where. Let's say that you've been learning about English history. You've done a little bit on William the Conqueror and you know that Richard of York and Henry Tudor were involved with the Wars of the Roses. And then of course there was the 100 Years' War after Charles IV died. But how do they **all link** together? Mind Maps are **the** tool of choice to help you see the **big picture** and **remember** who was who and when.

The Kings and Queens of England

Look at the list of Kings and Queens opposite. Get your paper and pens and draw a **Mind Map** to remember them all. Start by drawing a **main branch** for each of the different houses, or family names. Add what you know about each King or Queen to the Mind Map to help you **remember** who was who.

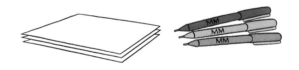

THE KINGS AND QUEENS OF ENGLAND

HOUSE OF NORMANDY

William the Conqueror . .1066–1087

William II 1087–1100

Henry I 1100–1135

Stephen 1135–1154

HOUSE OF THE PLANTAGENETS

Henry II 1154–1189

Richard I 1189–1199

John 1199–1216

Henry III 1216–1272

Edward I 1272–1307

Edward II 1307–1327

Edward III 1327–1377

Richard II 1377–1399

HOUSE OF LANCASTER

Henry IV 1399–1413

Henry V 1413–1422

Henry VI 1422–1461

HOUSE OF YORK

Edward IV 1461–1483

Edward V 1483

Richard III 1483–1485

HOUSE OF TUDOR

Henry VII 1485–1509

Henry VIII 1509–1547

Edward VI 1547–1553

Mary I 1553–1558

Elizabeth I 1558–1603

HOUSE OF STUART

James I 1603–1625

Charles I 1625–1649

Charles II 1660–1685

James II 1685–1688

William III with 1688–1702

    Mary II 1688–1694

Anne 1702–1714

HOUSE OF HANOVER

George I 1714–1727

George II 1727–1760

George III 1760–1820

George IV 1820–1830

William IV 1830–1837

HOUSE OF SAXE-COBURG-GOTHA

Victoria 1837–1901

Edward VII 1901–1910

HOUSE OF WINDSOR

George V 1910–1936

Edward VIII 1936

George VI 1936–1952

Elizabeth II 1952–

Kings & Queens of England Mind Map

066-87

I

William

NORMANDY

William II 1087-1100

Henry I 1100-35

Stephen 1135-54

1154-89 II Henry Richard

PLANTAGENETS

John 1199-1216

Henry III

Richard 1216-72

1377-99 Edward I 1272-1307

LANCASTER Edward

Edward II 1307-27

III

1327-77

Henry IV

Henry 1399-1413

Henry V 1413-22

YORK VI 1422-61

Edward IV 1461-83

Edward V 1483

Richard III

1483-85

EENS

nd

Catching your Dreams

We all dream at night, it's just that we don't always remember in the morning. Dreaming (and daydreaming) are the **best** when it comes to setting your **imagination free**. The more you can remember your dreams, the more you will help your **imagination** and get that memory of yours working to the max. Mind Maps are the **perfect** way to help you catch your dreams.

Keep pens and a notebook by your bed. When you go to bed at night, spend a minute or two thinking about dreaming.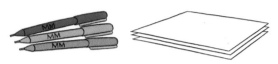
Repeat to yourself, '**I will remember my dreams**'. When you wake up in the morning, resist leaping straight out of bed. Try to lie still and stay sleepy. Think in a lazy sort of way about what's going round your head. Do you have an **image** of something in your mind? A feeling? Words?

As you lie still, bits of your dreams should start to come back. Get your **Mind Map pad** and draw a Mind Map of what you can remember so far. Drawing a **Mind Map** should help to jog your memory and you will find that you can remember **more** than you first thought.

BRAIN FLEXOR
HANDY HINT
Are you left-handed or right-handed? Just because you are one or the other, don't get stuck in a rut and use one hand more than the other. Brush your teeth, comb your hair or eat your food with the hand you don't normally use. Tie your shoes laces by starting with the loop in your other hand, change hands when you throw and catch balls, doodle with your non-writing hand – or with both! Keep swapping between hands when you do everyday things and you will make **BOTH** sides of your brain and body as **STRONG** as each other.

MOVE 'N' GROOVE TO YOUR FAVOURITE TUNE!
If you want to learn a new dance routine to your favourite
tune, do this by recording a Memory Movie of it in your head
and then with your body. If you go through it first in your
head it will be much easier to get the moves right
when you practise with your body.

Keep your dream Mind Maps to see if there is a **pattern** to your dreams. You
can learn **a lot** about yourself from them! Turn over the page to see the kind
of dream Mind Map you could draw. Can you imagine what this person was
dreaming about?

What time was it
when Sir Lancelot
looked at his
belly button?

The middle of
the knight!

My Dream Mind Map

straight
long
silent
CORRIDOR
white bright
shapes
walk
door
end
huge handle cold shiny
me moving with
people?
talking not
down

DOOR
open ledge narrow stone yellow
clear sky forest below
blue sun smell trees
bright noise HUGE! tops
hot earth
damp birds tigers green
exotic monkeys

The Master of Your Memory

Congratulations! Now that you have
mastered the magic memory tools in this book
you will be the master (or mistress!)
of your memory and the master of yourself. Keep
playing with your memory and it will reward you
by remembering everything
you want it to. And the most important
thing to remember of all?

There are no limits to how much you
can learn and remember, which means there
are no limits to what you can achieve!

The Mind Maps and Memory Tools you have learnt to use are as **powerful** as any magic wand.

They will be your friends for the rest of your life, and will help you, as you now know, to remember better, to concentrate, to be less stressed, to amaze your teachers, ace your exams and impress your friends. You know how brilliant **you** can be.

You are joining a growing club of millions of people around the world who are using Mind Maps and memory techniques to make them successful.

They will keep you ahead in every situation so you can go out and make the most of your **brainpower** and **get the grades** – and the life you – **deserve**.

BUZAN CENTRES

For information on all Buzan products and courses:
email: Buzan@BuzanCentres.com
website: www.BuzanCentres.com

UK:
Buzan Centre Ltd Headquarters
54 Parkstone Road
Poole
Dorset BH15 2PG

Tel: +44 (0) 1202 674676
Fax: +44 (0) 1202 674776

USA:
Buzan Centre USA Inc. (Americas)
P.O. Box 4
Palm Beach
Florida 33480

Free Toll in USA: +1 866 896 1024
Tel: +1 734 207 5287

Make the most of your mind today

Index